Believe

UPLIFT

GIVE

OFFER

Love

Affirm

Encourage

Elevate

Inspire

Share

Believe

Uplift

Give

Offer

Love

Affirm

Encourage

Elevate

Inspire

Validate

Share

Also by DeAnne Flynn

The Time-Starved Family:
Helping Overloaded Families Focus on What Matters Most

WHY EVEN OUR SMALLEST EFFORTS MATTER

DeAnne Flynn

DESERET
BOOK

SALT LAKE CITY, UTAH

Visit us at DeseretBook.com

Library of Congress Cataloging-in-Publication Data
Flynn, DeAnne W.
  The mother's mite : why even our smallest efforts matter / DeAnne Flynn.
    p. cm.
  Includes bibliographical references.
  ISBN 978-1-60641-937-3 (paperbound)
  1. Mothers—Religious life. 2. Mormon women—Religious life. 3. Motherhood—Religious aspects—The Church of Jesus Christ of Latter-day Saints. 4. Motherhood—Religious aspects—Mormon Church. 5. Child rearing—Religious aspects—The Church of Jesus Christ of Latter-day Saints. 6. Child rearing—Religious aspects—Mormon Church. I. Title.
  BX8641.F59 2011
  248.8'431—dc22   2010040575

Printed in the United States of America
R. R. Donnelley, Crawfordsville, IN

10   9   8   7   6   5   4   3   2   1

To my unsinkable mother,
for her extraordinary example of faith and resilience

Contents

Acknowledgments

ords could never adequately express my deep and heartfelt appreciation to all of the wonderful women who have contributed to this collection of stories, thoughts, and inspirations—as well as to my life personally. At the very top of this list is my supremely selfless mother, Carol, who constantly amazes me with her love. Many thanks to my gifted friends at Deseret Book. To my product director, Jana Erickson, for her remarkable patience and expertise. To Laurel Christensen, managing director of Time Out for Women, for her impeccable skill and sensitivity. To Leslie Stitt, multi-talented editor; Shauna Gibby, designer-extraordinaire; and Rachael Ward, typesetting whiz . . . Bravo! Many thanks to my fabulous TOFW colleagues: Tennisa Nordfelt, Angela Folsom, Christa Morgan, Chrislyn Barnes-Woolston, Laura Korth, Mary Moore, and Pat Williams. You all helped to make each event come together so seamlessly. My sincere gratitude to Sheri Dew for her faith and trust . . . again. And to Dianne, Glenn, Ashley, Liz, Sicely, Allyson, Jeanette, Suzy, Trish, Kelly, Sara, Annette, and Andrea—you have inspired me. I genuinely value your stories. A special thanks to Judi Bourne, Katie Graham, Emily Freeman, and Anne-Marie Barton for unselfishly sharing your own language. Loads of love to all those who were willing to reflect upon my questions and then share various life events for the benefit of other women, whom you will likely never meet. Your generosity is commendable. Thanks to my kind and supportive mother-in-law, Sylvia, and to my darling adopted mother, JoAnne. You are both mothers to be admired. I also offer genuine gratitude to my big-hearted husband. Without his help, I could not possibly have written this book. I love and adore you, Craig. And to my terrific "Lucky Seven"—Nicholas, Kate, Sarah, Jake, Jenny, Michael, and Elizabeth—you are the reason I aspire to be a better mother. I hope these ideas will help you in *your* parenting efforts someday.

To good women willing to share, I would sincerely value your support of *The Mother's Mite Initiative*, a worldwide, web-based gathering place to affirm, sustain, and celebrate those who mother. Thank you for offering your inspiring personal stories of hope—your own little "mother's mites"—with other thoughtful women at www.MothersMite.com.

Because we each need all the help we can get . . .

Introduction: On Offerings

believe most mothers, regardless of where we do our laundry or kneel to pray on this expansive globe, are inherently *givers*. This belief has been reaffirmed to me time after time, since every nurturer I know seems to exemplify remarkable altruism. Yet not one of the brave women I admire would ever tell you they're changing the world . . . albeit one child at a time. And why? Because we mothers tend to downplay our enormously vital responsibilities—often describing them as just "no big deal."

But mothering is a very big deal.

In fact, it is a rare woman who truly comprehends the *immensity* of motherhood before jumping in. Few of us initially grasp the fact that by choosing to become mothers, we are not only opting for a highly diverse range of job descriptions, we are also selecting a highly diverse life—one filled with unexpected bumps, peaks, valleys, and many tight turns. But it seems no matter which of the wonderful and varied stages of motherhood we are currently experiencing, there is at least one constant. And that's questioning ourselves.

One minute we mothers are questioning if we're doing enough for our children, and the next we find ourselves questioning if we're doing too much! Most of us are especially concerned with what we could or should be doing to prepare these up-and-coming adults for the bigger, long-term picture, yet we tend to discount or underestimate our contributions to the less exciting, daily grind.

Take a moment to recall the beloved New Testament story of the selfless woman who offered up her memorable widow's mites. In two brief accounts, the Apostles Mark and Luke describe the superficially minuscule contribution made by this humble woman who possessed such great faith that she gave "all her living" in order to wholly honor her God.

> And there came a certain poor widow, and she threw in two mites, which make a farthing. And he called unto him his disciples, and saith unto them, Verily I say unto you, That this poor widow hath cast more in, than all they which have cast into the treasury (Mark 12:42–43).

Now, let's take a little closer look at this seemingly simple story. It was Passover. The temple court was no doubt crowded and chaotic. As Jesus sat teaching beyond the inner court of the temple, He noticed an impoverished woman approaching one of the trumpet-shaped vessels supplied for the charitable contributions of worshippers. Ahead of this poor woman had been several proud, wealthy people who had thrown large sums of money into the vessels—which had probably made a loud and very obvious sound for all to hear. But as this widow approached, Jesus discerned the hearts of those in the tithing procession. He called to His disciples and pointed to the woman, saying, "This poor widow hath cast more in, than all they which have cast into the treasury"—even though she had only given two mites, the smallest coins then in circulation throughout Palestine.

Obviously, this committed woman believed in great miracles and trusted that God would somehow provide. And she must have made her offering out of love, rather than a need for external praise or recognition, since her contribution seems so very unimpressive on the surface. Notably, more than two thousand years later, this simple story is still being told and retold throughout all of Christianity to illustrate the type of faith and unselfishness we would each do well to develop. Now, *that* is worth pondering!

There is a similar story (though rarely told) about another generous woman who also sought to make a charitable offering . . .

And there came a certain weary woman and she threw in two frozen pizzas, which made a meal. And her husband did call unto him their children and saith unto them, "Verily, I say unto you, your compassionate mother hath cast more into the oven than you have." And they did value her offering because they knew she did give it unto them with all the energy she had left on that exceedingly taxing eve. Therefore, providing dinner for her family at that arduous hour was indeed . . . a mother's mite.

Not surprisingly, you won't find this version in your Bible! But we can draw some pretty interesting parallels from these two stories.

How similar to these women is each of us who wholeheartedly seeks to give—only to realize that our offerings are nothing short of meager. And, like them, we just might become tempted to compare our contributions to those of others, seeing ours as mere pittances—almost futile—when judged against the grand offerings of so many seemingly more able all around us.

Today, thanks to ever-present media and our often-competitive lifestyles, there is a universal misconception that bigger is somehow better; that life is just spontaneously superior for the woman next door. But, over time, I have come to realize that it's very often the little things that make the biggest difference in our lives and the lives of our family members. It's those outwardly insignificant things we usually take for granted, such as helping our families begin a brand new day with warm, fluffy pancakes in the early morning hours, or providing clean, soft pillows for them to sleep on at night. And these are just *two* of the seemingly insignificant things—or small mother's mites—we can give to promote a feeling of love and comfort in our homes.

For you, a mother's mite might be sharing a quiet moment with your children while drinking hot cocoa after shoveling snow, or pointing out the Big Dipper while laying on your back lawn at night, or playing board games with your family around the kitchen table. These moments are the precious stuff life is made of.

While many fortunate women seem to be drenched in such moments, others of us find them difficult to generate—or even to simply recognize.

It's puzzling that we mothers, grandmothers, leaders, and caregivers, regardless of how generous or unselfish we become, rarely catch sight of how truly significant we are in the moment-making process! We are all too tempted to view our ordinary, daily contributions as an endless string of undersized tasks, none of which seems at all worthy of any special consideration.

But they are.

Early in my motherhood, I often resisted fully answering my husband's well-meant question around dinnertime, "So, what did you do today?" I avoided articulating what I sensed would seem trivial, not because I was ashamed of my duties, but because I felt the minutia of my day-to-day life seemed much too minor to even mention. With exciting highlights such as changing diapers, cleaning up spills, doing multiple loads of laundry, and driving carpools, I often failed to recognize that I had actually accomplished something enormously worthwhile by the end of each day—no matter how many dirty dishes were still stacked in my kitchen sink.

I had mothered.

Yet, ironically, instead of consistently being pleased with my daily efforts, I somehow tended to concentrate on my undone tasks—on those areas that desperately needed improvement.

Without question, I was buying into that familiar fallacy that my offerings had to be grand to be great, and that small meant insignificant. But over the years I have come to realize that what I thought at the time were merely minor gestures, given affectionately to my children without a great deal of thought or planning, were actually little mother's mites. They were pint-sized gifts that my children have not only chosen to remember, but to cherish. And why are they cherished? Because these small offerings are evidence of my adoration and concern for each one of them—proof that my family members have always been and continue to be essential to me.

Most mothers do these things on a continual basis, usually without ever realizing it. As a matter of fact, there are undoubtedly women from Kentucky to Kenya offering little mother's mites at this very moment. Since these warm gestures may not always feel especially important at the time they are given, it might take years for us to learn just how much these seemingly ordinary contributions mattered in the lives of those we love.

And so, from one devoted nurturer to another, I warmly pass on this collection of small and simple offerings shared by the wonderful women in my life (although many of their names have been changed to protect the guilty). I hope these little snippets of affection will inspire you to recognize that even your smallest efforts do not go unnoticed . . . or unappreciated.

Enjoy!

"I remember my mother's prayers and they have always followed me. They have clung to me all my life."

Abraham Lincoln

1
Teacups

hen I was a child, visiting my Grandma Wilma in her lovely, well-kept home was always a treat. She was a slow and steady woman, with sadly declining health. But she proudly, and consistently, won blue ribbons at the county fair for her remarkable roses.

Whenever I'd come, she'd set out a vase and some kitchen shears by the back door. This was the signal that I could cut and arrange her stunning beauties for the dining room table. Hummingbirds danced around the sugar-sweetened feeders placed throughout her yard as I meticulously chose which roses would become part of my carefully crafted centerpiece.

My grandmother taught me to cut each rose at an angle, allowing the stems to drink freely from the medicine-laced water in my vase. "Drop one aspirin tablet into the water," she reminded me. "It will help keep your roses looking and smelling elegant for days."

She was a masterful cook and loved to prepare delicious meals for her family. I was always allowed to help in the kitchen, and I took great pleasure in cutting out biscuits and filling small bowls with jam, pickles, and other condiments for the table.

In the early afternoon hours following lunch, my Grandma Wilma would pull out her old Scrabble board, a dictionary, and two pads of paper—along with a new box of chocolates she'd purchased for such occasions. And there we would sit, playing Scrabble and eating chocolates. Although she was a literary, well-read woman, through some miraculous stroke of luck, I would somehow *win* every round! Then, she would retire to her oversized chair and cross-stitch while I prepared our sacred ritual—a time-honored, grandma-granddaughter tea party.

You see, my grandmother collected teacups. In fact, her friends gave her teacups from all over the world. She had several shelves of intricate, colorful cups. And she could remember the stories behind each meaningful one. I listened to these stories as I cautiously poured "tea" (usually peppermint tea or hot chocolate) and plopped sugar cubes into our fancy china cups with a silver spoon and a swish.

None of her cups matched one another, which made selecting just the right ones even more challenging. But my grandma let me choose. That was my job. I remember musing about the fact that she trusted me so implicitly to handle some of her most prized possessions. Yet she never cautioned me to be careful. I knew these fragile cups were precious to her. And here I was, a young girl, moving them all around. So risky was this business of retrieving them from the shelves, using them, cleaning them, and putting them away. But she never acted uneasy or insecure with my efforts.

My Grandmother Wilma's supreme confidence in me sent the powerful message, "You are a mature and responsible girl, and I trust you completely." To this day, I believe her confidence in me has had a profound impact in shaping my self-perception.

I am grateful to say that my grandmother left many of those priceless teacups in my care when she passed away years ago. And today, my own daughters have followed the long-standing tea party tradition, using those very same cups. I believe my Grandmother Wilma is now tickled and honored by her loving legacy. Interestingly enough, my girls have also had a hard time choosing which teacup to use on any given day.

My sentimental husband once suggested that the girls really shouldn't be using them at all, as he feared those dear antique teacups might accidentally get chipped or broken. But I've decided to "pass" on worrying and, instead, pass on my sweet grandmother's gift of *trust*. Because this is a mother's mite she so lovingly entrusted to me.

The Offering

Trust

An assured reliance on the character, ability, or strength of a person; confidence which is placed in someone.

Visit a lonely neighbor with your children.

Read fairy tales together by candlelight.

"My mom always says, 'I'm in love with you' instead of 'I love you.' That one little thing makes me feel like our relationship is cool and very unique."

Sarah, age 16

2
"Thick and Thin" Mothers

ne crisp autumn evening, while speaking in a southern state, I met a remarkable woman named Susanne. She was a Christian, married, but unable to have children of her own. So she determined to find opportunities to "mother" those around her. And one of those mothering opportunities came by volunteering in her community through the local chapter of the Boys and Girls Club.

Susanne was happily assigned to mentor a beautiful teenage girl who was being raised solely by her father. And because this young woman had seen some very turbulent times during her early years of life, she had plenty of both baggage and attitude. Even though Susanne was not the girl's biological mother, and certainly didn't deserve the treatment this troubled teen often dished out, she stuck by this girl's side through thick and thin. She listened to, hauled around, often fed, and supremely loved this girl—even when the teen's behavior was decidedly unlovable.

Though Susanne could have walked away at any time, she chose to stay . . . because she was a mother. A *mother?* you ask. But Susanne was unable to give birth. This wise and wonderful woman soon realized that merely "giving birth" does not a mother make. And while she never tried to replace this teenage girl's biological mother, Susanne wanted to consistently be there for the girl in every maternal way possible.

I've heard it said that some women give birth and never really mother, while other women never give birth and mother all of their lives. And I believe it's true. Take Mother Teresa, for example. Though she never gave birth to a child of her own, she spent her entire life mothering the poor, sick, aged, dying, or orphaned throughout India and other countries of the world. Born in 1910 as Agnes Gonxha Bojaxhiu, this Albanian Catholic nun became known as the "Saint of the Little Ways" because she believed in doing the little things in life well and with great love. (Sound familiar?) This small woman had an enormous heart. And through her organizations, she has cared for literally tens of thousands of people and her influence has been felt by hundreds of millions.

I have personally known many women who have opened their homes and hearts to the motherless children of the world. Several of my dearest friends have dreamed dreams about children in distant lands, only to search the world until those little ones were brought safely into their care. Others have found children in need nearby. But in each unique instance, it has been miraculous to watch these stories of love unfold.

Every time a child is nurtured here on earth it is sweet evidence that God, the Father of us all, is mindful of His children individually. Isn't it humbling to realize that He uses *us*—simple, imperfect women—as His hands here on earth, whether we've actually given birth to those we mother or not?

My friend, Nancy, was adopted as a child. Recently, she and her husband also decided to adopt. And though Nancy had already given life to two healthy children, she and her husband gave the gift of new life to a child in need of a stable home. This treasured little girl is now blessed with a loving family, and this family is now blessed with even greater love and purpose.

We are *all* mothers, really, whether we've actually given birth or simply cared for another human being. And through our charity and compassion, we can—*and will*—change lives . . . especially our own.

The Offering

Nurturance

A charitable interest in others; affectionate care; giving loving attention.

Go fly a kite—with your son.

Go take a hike—with your daughter.

"I appreciate my mom. She helps me iron my Sunday clothes. I'm actually not a very big fan of ironing. I know that sounds hard to believe."

Jake, age 14

3
The Coolest Date

here once was an unusually astute mother who knew the surest way to her two boys' hearts. Through food? Not really. Sports? You're getting closer. One particular sport? I guess you could call it that. Believe it or not, this perceptive mom thought the surest way to her young boys' hearts was through WWF wrestling!

Were her sons big fans? No, they were more than just big fans. They were WWF *fanatics*. So, when she heard that the WWF wrestlers were coming to her hometown, she immediately purchased three tickets to the event. One for each of her sons, and a third ticket for her.

Now, you may be asking yourself, "Did she also enjoy WWF wrestling? Really? Truly?" And the sincere answer to your question would be a resounding "Heavens, no." She would much rather have spent her hard-earned money on ballet or symphony tickets, movie tickets, or even dry cleaning tickets. But because she valued making memories with her sons while they were young and willing, she went to the wrestling event enthusiastically. Well, almost enthusiastically.

Perhaps the most amusing thing about the whole wrestling date with her boys was *their* take on it. Now, as adults, these sons both fondly recall sitting ringside with their mother, eating popcorn, watching the sweat and threats, hearing the growling and howling, admiring the splendor and spandex—while clearly thinking to themselves, "Wow, I'll bet Mom is just *digging* this right now! I'll bet she's just having the *greatest* time here with us."

Well, honestly? She was. Because she was spending time with her boys, doing something the boys both loved to do, eating delicious kernels of popped corn (which was something she loved to do) and making memories together as a family. And what mother wouldn't have treasured that wrestling match?

(Wait . . . you're not obligated to answer that.)

The Offering

Great Memories

Special moments or events a person can remember and fondly recall from the past.

WRESTLING POPCORN

The reason our family likes to call this recipe "Wrestling Popcorn" is because our children get to mix the caramel topping into the popcorn by wrestling it all together in a large paper bag. And it's not only fun to make—it's scrumptious to eat.

1 cup light corn syrup
2 cups brown sugar
½ cup butter
1 (14-ounce) can sweetened condensed milk
3 gallons popped popcorn (We have found that the prepopped buttered popcorn you can buy in huge bags at the grocery store works best)

1. Combine corn syrup, brown sugar, and butter in a medium saucepan.
2. Stirring regularly, bring to a boil—238 degrees F. on a candy thermometer—and then remove from heat.
3. Stir in sweetened condensed milk, mix thoroughly, and pour the mixture over the popcorn.
4. Then shake it up, baby!
   Having the popcorn in a large, clean paper bag coated with nonstick cooking spray is best. That way your children can mix the ingredients all together by attacking the bag! (Less mess = more fun, at least for me.)

Take a long walk with your teenager.

Rent a tandem bike on a sunny day.

"I wish my grandma actually lived with us, because she's the only person who loves princesses as much as I do."

Catherine, age 7

4
Watching at the Window

My dear friend and neighbor, Glenn, whose parents both died before he graduated from high school, remembers his own special mother with great admiration. She raised ten children, six of whom were boys. Glenn's father worked exceptionally hard for very little, often leaving for work between 4:00 and 5:00 A.M. while his mother stayed at home to care for the children. Although my friend was raised in a large family, he certainly didn't feel unnoticed. And since he was the youngest child, he was frequently alone with his mother as she went about her day.

He fondly recalls the small rituals they shared, such as playing cards at the kitchen table late into the evenings, counting down the New Year with a "toast" at midnight, and playing "The Numbers Game" where she would give him double-digit math problems to tally in his mind as quickly as he possibly could. (The answers to which she, herself, wasn't completely sure of!) This hardworking mom was definitely busy, but not too busy to notice her son's talent for mathematics.

Yet the mother's mite that clearly stands out for my friend was having his mom watch him at the window as he walked to the bus stop each morning for school. Simply knowing she was there, watching him march down the street, made all the difference to him—both then and now. "She didn't do it because she lacked trust in me, or because she didn't think I was capable. She did it because she loved me," Glenn tenderly explained.

Glenn's wife, Dianne, adopted this sweet custom while raising their own six children. Dianne chose to add a small wave and a smile as her children looked back toward the window, but the message was still identical: "I love you and I care about you as you start your new day." It's interesting that the ordinary so often becomes the extraordinary when it's motivated by love.

Maya Angelou once noted, "People will forget what you said . . . but people will never forget how you made them feel."[1]

Today, my friend Glenn not only remembers much of what his mother did, and many of the little things she said, but most important—he remembers how her comforting custom of watching him at the window made him feel. And that was *loved*.

The Offering

Comforting Custom

A repeated or long-established practice; a loving habit with an individual.

Jump in puddles with your two-year-old.

Sing to your baby.

"A mother's stories are like fairy gold—the more she gives away, the more she seems to have."

Robin, age 39 (and holding)

5
Fuzzy Slippers

y mother has always been a particularly clean domestic diva. In fact, she used to vacuum our carpets each and every morning wearing large, fuzzy house slippers. When I was old enough to walk, I began standing on top of these slippers, holding on to my mother's legs as she moved. She would walk ever so slowly, bending every now and then to reach a tricky spot as I practically did a backbend to remain attached.

I remember peeking my head through her knees, feeling like an acrobat as I wobbled and swayed unsteadily. I loved the uncertainty of this ritual—wondering if I would have the skill and balance to hold on, or if I would simply choose to let go and tumble to the ground with my mother's soothing words, "Come on, sweetie, get back on the horse," melting into my little heart and ears. It was a game, for sure, but it was also a gift to me since I loved being so close and connected to her.

Now, you need to understand that my mother is both ambitious and efficient. So the very fact that she would overlook greater proficiency for a greater priority was truly remarkable—especially now that I understand what it's like to care for a home, a husband, and children all at the same time. (And time is an exceptionally precious commodity.)

After vacuuming my own rugs more times than I'd care to admit, it's hard to imagine that my mother allowed me to do this balancing routine day after day, since having me along for the ride obviously slowed her down. But I am eternally grateful that my mother's priority wasn't speed or efficiency . . . it was me.

The Offering

Attention

A selective focusing of consciousness; a consideration of the needs and wants of another.

Add some rich, velvety chocolate to your daughter's glass of milk.

Mend a seam in your son's favorite pair of old sweats.

"I like taking a bath with my mom in our swimsuits. She says she's fat, but she's not. Only her tummy is."

Lizzie, age 4

6
Goddess in Training

To understand my friend Mary, you would simply have to meet her mother.

"Outrageous" is an understatement. This is a woman who has taken *layering* to a whole new level! In fact, to look at her at any given moment, you would think she was wearing every article of clothing she has ever owned—even in the summer.

But if you were to ask Mary's mother what she loves most, it wouldn't be clothing. No. Her husband, her daughter, and her costume jewelry, large hats, French perfume, and silky sheets would definitely be near the top of her list.

But not at the *very* top.

If you had the great fortune of meeting this singular woman, words such as "eccentric," "extreme," and "kooky" just might cross your mind. But the irony is that she is none of these things on the inside. We are so often tempted to judge one another by outer appearances, but one's trimmings and trappings are frequently misleading since they don't accurately reflect the depth of one's heart.

You see, when Mary's mother was a young girl she led a very meager and sheltered life. So, instead of facing her lackluster reality, she chose to live vicariously through novels, magazines, and anything she deemed exotic. She worked hard, earned money, and learned to sew—creating one-of-a-kind clothing and jewelry that satiated her immense appetite for self-expression through personal style.

As a young mother, she shared this flamboyance with her small daughter, who grew to relish her mother's attention and taste for the unexpected. Together, they make a lively pair, often matching their fashions right down to the nail polish.

These women collect dolls, china dishes, antique clocks, and anything baroque. They portray a zest and enthusiasm for life and acceptance of others that is nothing short of contagious.

These women consistently look for the "one"—reaching out to the homeless, the lonely, the heartbroken, and the lost. They are quick to act and slow to judge, serving in quiet ways that are known only to the recipients of their loving kindnesses. I have personally been the beneficiary of their uncommon concern and can honestly attest that there are no two people on earth quite like them!

The Offering

Zeal

An enthusiastic devotion to a cause, ideal, or goal and tireless diligence in its furtherance.

I have always admired Mary's utterly unique mother, not only because she shares an inseparable bond with her daughter, or because she drives a sassy red convertible with a bumper sticker that reads "Goddess in Training," but because the most important thing in the life of Mary's mom is her close and enduring connection with our Savior. He is her acknowledged Master, and her life is a living reflection of His love.

Listen to the rain
with your little ones.

Share your childhood memories.

"Night games with the neighborhood kids were usually played on our front lawn since my mom rocked at Kick the Can and Freeze Tag. She was the fastest runner on the block . . . and all the kids knew it."

Brad, age 39

7
Frosting Flowers

Even as a very young girl, I remember recognizing the safe, warm feeling I had while in the home of my Grandmother Olcott. She lived in a small, rural town where women wore curlers in their hair to the grocery store on Saturday afternoons and gathered eggs in their backyard chicken coops before breakfast. This was a place where people *knew* one another—where your neighbor's success or heartache was also your own.

My grandmother drove the school bus in this town for more than thirty years, so each and every child within a twenty-mile radius of her route was known by name and loved. One by one, on weekdays at eight and again at three, children were individually greeted as they entered the large mechanical door of my grandma's yellow school bus, where she always had a cheerful smile to share, as well as a kind word or a small piece of candy. The kids all recognized that my grandmother's heart was every bit as big as her steering wheel, so they respected her and did their best to stay in line. Even the tough ones.

In addition to "driving bus," my grandma also helped my grandpa at their shoe repair shop on Main Street, did custodial work for the local church, and created custom-made wedding cakes—magnificent edible towers, stacked high with layers and layers of creamy, white icing. I remember watching her craft the intricate decorations for these marvelous masterpieces—exquisite flowers made of lightly colored frosting, and leaves that looked far too lovely to eat. She would stand by the window in her bright, sunny kitchen using the daylight to help her see every detail more clearly. But the most illuminating part to me was my grandmother's extraordinary patience as she let me practice making these charming flowers on my own.

As I ineffectively crafted blobs of gooey sweetness onto the long, metal instrument she used for spinning the petals, she would repeatedly encourage me to keep trying—even though I was obviously frosting-flower-impaired. My Grandmother Olcott never let me think of myself as a culinary klutz, although she may have secretly wondered if I had been switched at birth! She just overlooked my weakness, without judgment, and accepted me unconditionally. And I deeply valued that acceptance.

I remember her continual humming and singing as we worked together in her kitchen, singing songs like, "Mares eat oats, and does eat oats, and little lambs eat ivy. A kid'll eat ivy too, wouldn't you?" Whether we were decorating wedding cakes, bottling homegrown tomatoes, or peeling potatoes for dinner, my grandma talked about her upcoming projects and plans. She was without question an optimistic dreamer. But she was also a *doer*.

No project, assignment, or obstacle could stop my fearless grandmother in her tracks. She just plowed forward with a positive, confident attitude regardless of what she happened to be doing at that particular moment. Even with a husband who suffered through multiple hip surgeries, and a son who dealt with severe health problems in his youth, my grandmother got up each morning and expected only the best from every new day. She was a shining example of resilience and determination throughout her entire life.

In a world where most people are daily trying to escape from reality, my grandmother taught me to improve mine. And through her example of hard work and perseverance, I have learned that life is always as good as you make it.

The Offering

Optimism

An inclination to put the most favorable construction upon actions and events, to anticipate the best possible outcome.

FROSTED FLOWER COOKIES

Use refrigerated, prepared sugar cookie dough. Or make your own by combining the following:

1 cup butter or margarine, softened

½ cup sugar

2¼ cups all-purpose flour

2 teaspoons lemon extract or vanilla

¼ teaspoon salt

1 egg

1. Preheat oven to 400 degrees F. Beat butter and sugar in large bowl with electric mixer on medium speed until creamy, or mix with spoon. Stir in flour, extract, salt, and egg.
2. Place dough in cookie press or roll dough ¼-inch thick and cut with cookie cutters.
3. Bake 6 to 9 minutes or until set, but not brown. Immediately remove from cookie sheet to wire rack.
4. When cool, decorate and eat 'em up!

Butter Cream Frosting

    1 cup butter, room temperature

    3 cups powdered sugar

    2 teaspoons vanilla extract

    1 to 2 tablespoons milk or cream

1. In a mixing bowl, combine the butter with the powdered sugar using an electric mixer. Beat on low speed until sugar is moistened, then beat on medium-high speed for about 2 minutes.
2. Add the vanilla and 1 tablespoon of milk or cream and beat until smooth. Beat in more milk or cream as needed for spreading consistency.

This makes enough frosting for about 3 dozen cookies.

Preserve a small piece of yourself for generations to come.

Watch the sunrise on the roof with your seven-year-old.

"The fabulous thing about my mother was her knack for noticing the best in me. She always told me that I could do anything.

"And I believed her."

Mildred, age 85

8
Roots

everal years ago at Christmastime, my mother began a deeply meaningful custom. As a special gift for each one of my daughters, she wrapped a beautiful binder with the words "Family Memories" printed in big gold letters on the cover. Inside, she placed a personalized pedigree chart for each girl, along with a biography of a remarkable female ancestor.

The first woman my mother chose to write about was her great-great-grandmother, Flora Clarinda Gleason Washburn. Clarinda, as she was called, was born in the early 1800s in Massachusetts. When she was almost five years old, her parents moved to Ohio and, just sixteen days after their arrival, her mother died, leaving Clarinda, her three-year-old sister, and a two-week-old baby . . . motherless. Although her father remarried, Clarinda lived with relatives throughout much of her childhood.

As a young woman, Clarinda learned the art of dressmaking and also became a competent nurse. Between these two skills, she earned her living from a very early age. She became engaged to be married in her later teens, but her fiancé grew ill and, just prior to their wedding day, he died. Although he was gone, Clarinda lived with this young man's family for the next two years.

After finding the restored gospel, she moved to Illinois where an angry mob set fire to the home where she was staying with a friend. Everything Clarinda owned was burned—including all of her lovely, handmade dresses.

In 1846, Clarinda was married in Illinois. She and her new husband were among the first to leave Illinois in the trek west to the Rocky Mountains to escape further religious persecution. But as the group traveled west, her husband lagged behind and urged Clarinda to continue on with the company. He did not arrive in Winter Quarters with the others. As men rapidly built houses for their own families, a charitable man set out to build a shelter for Clarinda. However, Clarinda was still living in her wagon in January when her first child was born—a baby girl she named Huetta Clarinda.

Since there were no dressmaking opportunities, and nursing was done without cost, this resourceful mother went into the willow patches along the riverbanks and gathered willows, stripped off the bark, and wove them into fine baskets to trade for food and provisions for her journey. That spring, Clarinda joined a wagon company and drove her own mule team and wagon the entire way to the Salt Lake Valley, arriving on October 18, 1847, with her new baby daughter. Soon thereafter, she was granted a divorce.

In 1849, Clarinda had the courage to marry once more. Her husband, Abraham

Washburn, was a good and kindly man of worthy character. They were soon called to establish a new settlement in Manti, Utah. But during their first winter there, all thirty of the cattle they had brought from the Salt Lake Valley died. While living in huts through deep snows and severe frosts, Clarinda regularly removed snakes from their living quarters. In the spring, she was finally given a home of her own.

Clarinda had six more children while living in Manti. She took in newly married couples from Denmark who had no place to live and could not speak English. She divided the room of her sturdy house with draperies, allowing the young couples to have their separate quarters until they could create their own homes. In addition, she and her daughters often baked large sacks of crackers for the men and teams to take along the trail when bringing immigrants to the West. They also took in soldiers during the Black Hawk War.

After many years, she and her

The Offering

Family Legacy

Something valuable handed down from the past.

family moved to the small settlement of Monroe, Utah, where there were no doctors at that time. Clarinda continued to help the needy, sometimes leaving her own sick children with her husband while she went out to help deliver new babies or care for those who were ill. To scores of grateful people, Clarinda was a savior, as well as a saint. She was a pioneer in the truest sense of the word.

My great-great-great grandmother, Flora Clarinda Gleason Washburn, worked with all her might to prepare the way for others and to improve conditions wherever she went. And following in her great-great-grandmother's footsteps, my own dear mother has also improved our family's conditions—helping us gain a greater understanding of our own roots by sharing accounts of the extraordinary women whose blood runs through our veins. By giving this considerate gift at Christmastime, we've all come to love our ancestral heritage and the sisterhood that binds us together as women of faith.

Snuggle your kids in their great-grandmother's quilt.

Frame photos of your children's ancestors.

"I like it when my mom takes me along on her errands. We get to talk, and we usually get berry smoothies."

Jenny, age 12

9
Pennies from Heaven

Most children who attend grade school somehow manage to become skilled at little juvenile chants such as, "One, two, skip a few, ninety-nine, one hundred," "Don't step on a crack or you'll break your mother's back," and "Bubble gum, bubble gum in a dish, how many pieces do you wish?" Well, one young girl truly *believed* what she'd learned on the playground about pennies bringing good luck, so she made a habit of looking for them often. ("Find a penny, pick it up, and all day long you'll have good luck.")

It amused her family, particularly her mother, that this young girl was so intent upon stumbling across fate that she would frequently keep her head down as she walked, being bound and determined to discover some unfettered good fortune in the form of a penny!

So one day, just minutes before the school bus pulled up to the neighborhood stop, bringing this young girl home from school, her mother scattered literally hundreds of brand new, shiny pennies all over the sidewalk by the bus stop. The mother had made a special trip to the bank earlier that afternoon to collect a large supply of polished pennies with the sole intent of bringing her daughter some much sought-after luck and delight.

Sure enough, at precisely the appointed time, her daughter's school bus pulled up to the stop where an unsuspecting bus driver swung the large doors wide open, revealing to the young girl a glistening, coppery sidewalk of providence! Spying from behind a tree, this thoughtful mother thrilled at her daughter's undeniable surprise and joy. She now had a whole pavement filled with "luck," in addition to having a mother who cared enough to create it for her. She turned out to be a very fortunate girl indeed.

The Offering

Sheer Delight

Something that gives great pleasure, a high degree of gratification, or extreme satisfaction.

Offer to chauffeur, just to know what's going on in your child's world.

Help your teen give a new mom some time alone.

"My mom was a talented shower singer. I loved to listen and laugh as she belted away in the mornings. She always helped me start my day with a smile."

Tom, age 48

10
Meteors past Midnight

fun friend of mine has a creative young family who has made watching for meteors a summertime tradition. Treating this amazing event like they would the Fourth of July fireworks, they lay blankets on their back lawn or sit in comfortable lawn chairs, spray on the bug spray, and eat treats as they stare eagerly into the night horizon. When a meteor suddenly appears to shoot quickly across the sky, they all "oooh" and "aaah" as if they could catch that falling star and put it in their pockets.

This resourceful family has made star gazing not only a fascinating hobby, but an increasingly essential part of countless warm weekend evenings from May through September. And since these spectacular shows are priced just right, they often invite friends and neighbors to attend their open-air backyard theater!

According to stardate.org, "'Shooting stars' and 'falling stars' are both names that people have used for many hundreds of years to describe meteors—intense streaks of light across the night sky caused by small bits of interplanetary rock and debris, called meteoroids, crashing and burning high in Earth's upper atmosphere. Traveling at thousands of miles an hour, meteoroids quickly ignite in the searing friction of the atmosphere 30 to 80 miles above the ground."[2] The approximate dates and times for these unconventional showers are all listed online at http://www.stardate.org/nightsky/meteors/.

Without a doubt, this highly unique and interesting activity makes for a memorable family night. It's definitely a "mother's mite" idea your children will appreciate and even treasure for years to come . . . and possibly even continue with their own families someday.

The Offering

Unusual Adventure

An exciting or remarkable experience; an uncommon or rare quest.

Host a free lemonade stand in your neighborhood.

Listen for crickets out on your back lawn.

"Our house wasn't always clean, but our faces usually were—thanks to my caring mom."

Laura, age 30

11
Birthday Pie

It's hard to say exactly how one of my favorite mother's mites began. Perhaps it all started because we had rhubarb plants growing spontaneously on the sides of our spring ditch in my backyard when I was young, with plenty of bright red strawberries just ready to pick in our garden. Or maybe it just blossomed out of my original experience with strawberry-rhubarb pie at age five, when I actually *devoured* my piece of pie while most of my cousins wouldn't take a single bite of theirs. However it initially happened, my mother was absolutely brilliant to start baking me a strawberry-rhubarb pie on my birthday each year because it has always been such a unique and highly appreciated gift.

One of the main things I adore about eating this odd-looking dessert is how the sweet, fluffy whipped cream offsets the tart, often sour taste of the rhubarb. My mom, flat out, makes the flakiest piecrust on the planet and uses only perfectly ripened strawberries. But, to be completely honest, a person simply must be *crazy* to like rhubarb—regardless of their upbringing. It's sort of like watercress. Or asparagus. You may think these gourmet delicacies are saved only for the finest restaurants until you've driven down the back roads of my hometown. These plants are just instinctively springing out of the earth around every pond bank and irrigation canal. They are certainly not served beside freshly made soufflés. They are simply served from the small town *ground!*

I'll never forget receiving an unexpected package one mild September day when I was living in New England in my early twenties. The FedEx man delivered a small box marked "fragile" that had been sent overnight from Seattle. And even though I had experienced many of my mother's fabulous pies on my birthday—and it just happened to be my birthday—I never imagined or expected her to seek out rhubarb, find some fresh strawberries, and bake me a pie while I was living on the opposite side of the country.

Now, does this sound like a "small and simple" thing to you?

To me, it would have been a monumental undertaking. But to my gastronomic mother, it was easy and uncomplicated. "It was nothing," she responded when I gushed in gratitude.

The Offering

Thoughtfulness

Anticipation of the needs and wants of others; heedfulness.

And do you know why it was no big deal for her?

Because she knew that pie would send a powerful message to me. A message that she loved me. That she was thinking about me. And that she cared about my special day. We women usually come wired that way, with a homing beacon for discovering the gifts that matter most to those we care about.

Even now, whether my mom is baking a pie for my birthday, helping one of my children with a special project, or just dropping by for a quick visit, she continually gives me the precious gift of her love. And that's the most meaningful gift of all . . .

"EASY AS PIE"

While strawberry-rhubarb birthday pie is definitely delicious, this delectable dessert will have your family begging for more . . . and it's so easy to prepare. Even a child can do it.

> 1 prepared pie crust, either Oreo or graham cracker (You can also tightly line the pie tin with ladyfinger cookies for the crust)
> 1 half gallon peppermint, chocolate chip, or cookie dough ice cream, softened
> Whipped cream (optional)
> Chocolate or caramel sprinkles/topping (optional)
> Maraschino cherries (optional)

1. Freeze pie crust until solid.
2. Fold softened ice cream into pie crust and spread evenly.
3. Freeze until ice cream is solid.
4. Top with whipped cream dollops, favorite toppings, and cherries (if desired).
5. Serve and enjoy!

There are as many variations to this recipe as there are people who prepare it. Experiment using your favorite flavors!

Teach your children proper table manners.

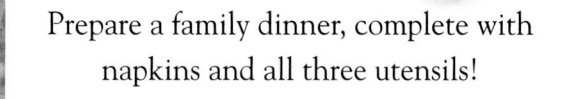

Prepare a family dinner, complete with napkins and all three utensils!

"I love it when my mom makes chocolate pudding parfaits.
She alternates layers of whipped cream and layers
of pudding—it looks super fancy."

Olivia, age 11

12
Picnics and Politics

While my friend Emily prepares a nutritious dinner on most evenings and gathers her family around the table—often reminding her children to chew with their mouths closed, to pass food instead of reaching for it, and to use their napkins instead of their sleeves—she makes some pretty big exceptions when it comes to election night. Sure enough, when the next leaders of our country are being determined, out come the picnic blankets and in come the kids, dinner in hand, to the family room—aka "Election Central." And it's not just any dinner, but a good, old-fashioned, American meal—slow-cooked barbeque ribs, baked potatoes, Brussels sprouts, and rolls. She even buys really fun drinks, a fancy dessert, and little munchies to last all night long.

Why does she go to all this work? Because Emily loves the entire political process, from getting to know the candidates to making sure every dangling chad is accounted for. She wants her children to grow up with a desire to vote and to be avid participants in the democratic process. So on election night she breaks two hard and fast family rules: you don't have to eat your food in the kitchen, and you can stay up until the last election results are in—even if it's all night long! "Election

Central" provides a great opportunity to teach about the election process, civic responsibilities, and the differences between each candidate's views. Opinions are shared and discussed as the map of the United States slowly fills in with blue and red states, respectively, according to the number of votes counted. It's a night her kids look forward to, filled with out-of-the-ordinary rules, out-of-the-ordinary food, and out-of-the-ordinary conversation . . .

. . . and that's just one of the many reasons why my friend Emily is truly an out-of-the-ordinary mom.

The Offering

Patriotism

A love for or devotion to one's country; national loyalty.

Go fish.

Celebrate holidays.

"My mom is the best at skiing because she doesn't need Edgie-Wedgies on her ski tips. She just skis without them real easy . . . and I follow in her tracks."

Ben, age 6

13
The Family Star

woman I genuinely admire has an illuminating ritual that reveals a great deal about her family's loving relationship. Whenever there is the slightest cause to rejoice, to mourn, or to lighten an emotional load—Kim simply turns on the star above her front door. And that star serves as a symbol to all who have eyes to see.

This story began when Kim's father-in-law was just a little boy growing up in humble circumstances. After visiting a lovely home with a bright, beautiful star all lit up at Christmastime, he vowed to have a home of his own with a lighted star right above the front door someday. And after many years of hard work, he realized his dream.

Today, all of his children—now with families of their own—respectfully display a star above their front doors year-round. For Kim, the star is a beacon. "When really hard things have happened in our family," she says, "I always light up the star. It represents hope. It's a symbol of Christ coming into the world and of Christ coming into our lives."

Kim also uses their family star as a symbol of celebration. "I light it when our children get married, when missionaries leave, when they come home, when new babies are born, when people succeed, or at times when family members truly need to feel loved. When they see the star above our door—they know that star shines just for them."

One evening, after her husband had a particularly difficult business meeting, Kim anticipated her husband coming home late and discouraged. Although she knew she couldn't change the sad events of his day, Kim knew she could turn on the star so he would see it as he drove up the street toward their home. "It makes me emotional just thinking about it," she sighed. And I'm certain it had a similar effect on her husband that night.

Kim loves giving stars to the people she cares about most, like to her missionary son when he was serving in Pennsylvania and to her newly married daughters as they started their own homes and new lives. And though there are certainly multiple layers of meaning behind this endearing

The Offering

A Significant Symbol

Something important that represents something else by association.

tradition, Kim feels the message that star conveys most meaningfully to the members of her family is, "You're going to be okay. We're here. Christ is here. We'll all get through this together."

And with such a loving and supportive mother, there's no doubt that they will.

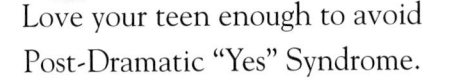

Learn to text, even though you may feel technologically challenged.

Love your teen enough to avoid Post-Dramatic "Yes" Syndrome.

"Once, when I was sick, my mom actually
got out the blow dryer and made my sheets
all cozy before I climbed into bed.

"Now that's love."

Kate, age 18

14
Magic Fingers

It wasn't the fact that his mom was an adult tennis champ, or was president of her state's medical auxiliary, or was well-read, or world-traveled, or witty that mattered to my husband, Craig. He really loved the fact that his mother would scratch his back whenever she was nearby.

Ever since he could remember, her heavenly back scratches would calm and relax him as he sat in church, watched a movie, or casually conversed after dinner with his family. Her long, thin nails were the perfect instruments to subdue even the most severe case of "the itchies." And her technique was unmatched. After she had begun one of her mesmerizing fingertip massages, my husband would go immediately into a trance—eyes glazed over and head free from worry.

When he was young, Craig would lay his head on her lap like a cozy kitten and practically start purring as her nails swirled and stroked his small neck and spine. There was nothing on earth more secure or serene than his mother's loving touch. For him, her hands held magic.

After all, they were the hands that cleaned off his little face and cooked all of his favorite foods. The hands that picked him up when he fell down and set him

"My grandma takes me on dates to the children's museum just because she really loves to be with me."

Elizabeth, age 7

15
Asparagus Soup

I t's fascinating that something as simple as dishing up a bowl of warm, creamy soup on a cool, dark evening can promote such a genuine glow in the faces around my home. But it does. In fact, little else speaks such fondness to my family as does making them asparagus soup—especially during the wintertime.

I usually make this family favorite on Sunday evenings (mainly because that's when I have cooked asparagus left over from dinner). And it's different every time I prepare it since following a recipe is so tedious to me. But my children will tell you that this dish will heal them when they're at death's door, warm them when they're frozen stiff, and remind them that they're loved immensely—by me.

After everyone has been apart for a while taking Sunday afternoon naps, reading, or just playing games, I pull out the asparagus and plug in the blender. It's amazing how that sound attracts our family to the kitchen.

My oldest son prefers this soup with larger pieces of asparagus, my husband likes it less thick, and everyone has a differing opinion about the amount of fresh ground pepper I add, but all nine of us agree on one thing—this soup tastes fabulous topped with cheese and buttery focaccia croutons. (What doesn't?)

As I stir the pot of creamy goodness and smell that moist, flavorful steam, I sometimes catch a small glimpse of becoming like Paula Deen—gathering my family around our hearth with delicious food, feeling ever so domestic, and loving every moment of it!

I once watched a Thanksgiving video clip on YouTube that captured the random responses of people on the streets of New York City around the holidays. When asked what he was truly grateful for, one man's immediate response was, "I'm thankful for macaroni and cheese. It's a very heartwarming thing for me because my mother used to make it for me every week when I was in kindergarten." Macaroni and cheese? On the surface, it's so very, very ordinary. I wonder if his mother ever imagined he would grow up and say, "I'm thankful for my mom because she made me mac and cheese when I was five years old!"

Watching that interview made me wonder how my now-small son might respond to the same question as a

The Offering

Nourishment

The act of nourishing, sustaining, and benefiting.

grown man. Will he even remember our Sunday evenings—gathered together in our kitchen and bonding over mugs of warm asparagus soup?

I certainly hope so.

Because our favorite soup isn't just made with cream and steamed asparagus.

It's also made with love.

CREAMY ASPARAGUS SOUP

This lip-smacking soup will help you use up all of your leftover asparagus. The recipe serves 6, so I double it for my family. Even kids love it!

1 pound cooked asparagus
6 tablespoons butter
6 tablespoons flour
5 cups chicken broth or equal amount of extra flavorful chicken base
1 cup heavy whipping cream (or half-and-half)
Salt and ground pepper

1. Run 1 pound cooked asparagus through a blender or food processor with a little water. Set aside.
2. In a large pot, melt butter and then stir in flour and blend well.
3. Add chicken broth (you can use part or all bouillon or chicken base).
4. Stir until well blended, cooking constantly until broth boils and starts to thicken.
5. Add cream or half-and-half, and then add asparagus, salt, and ground pepper to taste. (For more flavor, add extra bouillon or chicken base.)
6. Heat soup until hot, but not boiling. If it needs to be thickened, add a little cornstarch dissolved in water.
7. Top with grated cheese and/or seasoned croutons.

Make a plan.

Make a memory.

"My mother-in-law always made me feel like I was her favorite. But when she passed away, I was surprised to learn each one of her daughters-in-law felt that same way.

"This inspires me."

Donna, age 61

16
Nana's Bells

It's not the soft leather sofa or the flat-screen TV that draws Maggie's grandchildren like excited little butterflies to her sun-drenched study. It is most certainly her bells.

You see, many years ago when this eager grandmother's first grandchild was born, she began shopping for the perfect porcelain bell to represent the child's precious new life. This was to be the beginning of a longstanding ritual for Maggie, affectionately known by her grandchildren as "Nana." And from that day to this, each time a new baby is born into Maggie's close-knit family, she discovers just the right bell for that distinctive new child and places it upon the shelf next to all of the others.

While Maggie's bells are certainly eye-catching, and each one extraordinarily unique, there is definitely much more to those decorative accessories than might casually meet the eye. For Maggie's bells are actually her "goody guardians." They are keepers of her scrumptious small treats—such as chocolate-covered raisins, cashews, chewing gum, or little candies—which never cease to surprise and delight the children she loves most in the world when they come for a visit.

As they scurry through their Nana's front door and excitedly race to the large shelf in her study, each child carefully lifts his or her own bell to discover the tiny surprise tucked neatly inside. Occasionally, Maggie writes little love notes to grace her goodie gifts. But—note or not—whatever this creative grandmother's bells happen to be harboring on any given day always seems to be just enough to say "I love you" to those little ones who delight in peeking underneath to find a bit of magic waiting there just for them.

The Offering

Creative Fun

An activity that brings joy, amusement, or pleasure.

Start a new tradition.

Stop an old pattern.

"My mother gave me the greatest gift of all. She gave me the gift of uninhibited enthusiasm."

Bill, age 54

17
The Enchanted Dryer

ne of my oldest and most trusted friends claimed to have an enchanted clothes dryer. That's right, she was certain her dryer could magically awaken even the sleepiest children—especially in winter.

Her *dryer*, you say?

How could a clothes dryer wake a child? Was it noisy?

No, it wasn't the noise her dryer made that helped my friend's children practically raise from the dead before school each day. It was the anticipation of wrapping warm, comfortable clothing around their tired little bones that helped this woman rouse her drowsy crew in the early morning hours.

As inconvenient as it may sound, my friend simply made a habit of putting the clothing her children planned to wear that day into the dryer when she woke up in the morning. That way, each of them had nice warm clothes to put on as they started a brand new day. My friend always felt this single act spoke volumes to her children.

And apparently it did.

Now grown, these children still express, with great fondness, their love for their mother's enchanted dryer ritual. They've spoken of their deep devotion to her, never questioning her devotion to them. Getting out of bed at my friend's home always held the promise that there would be warmth just waiting there . . .

. . . and that warmth didn't emanate only from a clothes dryer.

The Offering

Consideration

Careful, kind,
deliberate thought or concern
for other people.

Smell the flowers.

Watch for birds.

"My mom makes me feel so important to her because she regularly asks for my opinion. That really means a lot to me."

Chelsea, age 17

18
Celebr-eight-ing the Moment

Katie will always remember a spontaneous gathering her mother once planned in honor of the calendar date 8/8/88. The idea grew out of the fact that the number eight had always held great significance for them since they had eight people in their family.

The kids in Katie's clan knew something unusual was up when they were all called home to eat dinner together without notice. Each of the many lessons, sports practices, and activities were quickly cancelled as her family members gathered around their kitchen table, still curious.

After greeting her puzzled family, this clever mother announced that she had placed eight beautiful flowers in the centerpiece, that she had made stir-fry with eight different, delicious ingredients, and that she would be serving ice cream with eight yummy toppings for dessert—all because the date 8/8/88 was so very great!

"It was rare that we had our dad home for dinner since he owned and operated a small retail business, but somehow he managed to sit at the head of our table that evening as we all enjoyed our little 'party' together," Katie fondly recalls. "The spontaneous nature of the evening and my mom's excitement and creativity really stand out in this memory for me. In her joy to give to us, we all felt joy ourselves."

I'll bet Katie's mother would never have dreamed that her efforts that day would eventually become one of her daughter's fondest thoughts and memories of life in her parents' home. It just goes to show, we never really know what will happen when we choose to make the effort.

The Offering

Effort

The use of physical or mental energy to do something; an earnest attempt; an achievement.

Take a break from your daily routine.

Give your children
the benefit of the doubt.

"Perhaps my mother's sweetest single act was listening to me. She was, and still is, a superb listener."

Craig, age 49

19
Cinnamon Swirl Bread

ears ago, when my friend's daughter was in college and came home for the weekends, my friend always offered her daughter a loaf of cinnamon swirl bread to take back to her apartment. Now, as a new mother living in a distant state, when this daughter is feeling homesick, she will simply buy a loaf of cinnamon swirl bread. My thoughtful friend mused that her girl had totally forgotten about all the cash she had handed out each weekend like an ATM machine. It was the cinnamon swirl bread she remembered most. "Who knew?" my friend mused. "I could have saved a lot of money!"

Isn't it fascinating that something as simple as a loaf of bread can provide peace and comfort to the aching heart of my friend's daughter? Of course, it isn't actually the *bread* that satisfies this woman (although one might argue that point—depending upon who baked it). It is surely the association of sweet bread with sweet memories that connects this young woman with her mother across the miles and gives her strength on difficult days.

You know, Dorothy was absolutely right: "There *is* no place like home." But as hard as it may be for many of us to accept, we mothers are merely trainers—preparing these sons and daughters of ours to confidently leave us. And the lessons we provide now, both large and especially small, will be the building blocks they'll use to steady their own walls and secure their own loose ties when the fierce winds blow.

Whether they are offered a loaf of cinnamon swirl bread or some other token of our love, the children we are blessed to nurture can thankfully find solace in remembering our small acts of kindness. Those gentle reassurances that help them know we are always there for them, even
when we're physically far away.

The Offering

Reassurance

The act of reassuring; restoring someone's confidence.

CINNAMON SWIRL BREAD

1⅓ cups sugar, divided

2 teaspoons ground cinnamon

2 cups all-purpose flour (or organic flour)

1 tablespoon baking powder

½ teaspoon salt

1 egg, beaten

1 cup milk

⅓ cup vegetable or canola oil

1. Preheat oven to 350 degrees F. Lightly grease a 9 x 5-inch loaf pan. In a small bowl, mix together ⅓ cup sugar and cinnamon; set aside.

2. In a large bowl combine flour, baking powder, salt, and remaining 1 cup sugar. Combine egg, milk, and oil in a separate bowl and then add to flour mixture. Stir until just moistened.

3. Pour half of the batter into the pan. Sprinkle with half the reserved cinnamon-sugar mixture. Repeat with remaining batter and cinnamon-sugar mixture. Swirl a knife through the batter to marble it.

4. Bake for 45 to 50 minutes, or until a toothpick inserted into center of the loaf comes out clean. Let cool in pan for 10 minutes before removing to a wire rack to cool completely. The loaf cuts best when it has been wrapped in foil overnight.

Listen more.

Worry less.

"My grandma makes the very best strawberry jam. She calls it 'red butter' since that's what I named it when I was two years old."

Michael, age 10

20
The Surprise Visit

hen my oldest children were very small and I was often very pregnant, my husband traveled a great deal. On one particularly lengthy business trip, I began to notice that the balanced meals I had once proudly prepared had gradually diminished to a rotating fare of macaroni and cheese, chicken noodle soup, pizza, and sliced apples while he was away.

And that wasn't all . . .

The tidiness of our family's once semi-organized abode had also sadly declined—considerably. After all, "Why would I bother putting the toys and art supplies away if I were just going to get them out again in a few hours anyway?" I reasoned, while the clutter around me just kept rising. Were we having fun together? Yes, indeed! Did the mess mean less stress for me? Absolutely. But the Play-Doh, puzzles, and piles were getting a bit out of hand—even for the most relaxed housekeeper.

It was about that time when my doorbell rang. While the unmistakable sound chimed out, I hesitated for just a brief moment, pretending I hadn't recognized what I feared I had heard. But any mother of young children will attest to the fact that "pretending" not to notice there is someone standing at your front door after the bell rings is like trying to ignore a fire siren at close range.

I shuddered.

"Oh, please let it be a salesperson," I prayed, as I moved reluctantly toward the door with multiple little bodies clamoring to see who would be waiting there.

As luck would have it, my mother- and father-in-law were standing there on my doorstep, smiling. They proceeded to tell me they were just in the neighborhood and thought they'd drop by for a little visit. Once again, I hesitated. The thought of opening the door any wider than a crack sent chills down my spine.

How petty.

How ridiculous.

How ultimately proud, you may be thinking to yourself.

Well, you would be right on all three counts because I *really* didn't want them to see me this way. I didn't want them to judge me or think that I was in over my head. But after a minute or

The Offering

Empathy

The capability to share or relate to another being's emotions and feelings.

two at the front door, they finally asked if they could come in. I reluctantly agreed, quickly explaining all the while that we were just not quite ourselves right then.

I'll never forget the look on my sweet mother-in-law's face as she perused my cluttered kitchen area and then giggled. After all, she was the mother of seven. And I'm sure she had seen some pretty good messes in her lifetime. But she never said a word about my disarray. She talked to my children, asked how I was, and caught up on all the latest news about our growing family.

From that day to this, I have remembered the gracious and nonjudgmental way she handled a potentially awkward situation. I knew she had walked a mile in similar moccasins. But after that experience, I also knew she understood the blisters that tend to come and go along the way.

Hug your grandchildren.

Let your daughter-in-law be your
daughter-in-love.

"When I was in junior high, my mom used to drive
my buddies and me around in her big old minivan. We all thought
she was the coolest mom for letting us crank up the radio."

Doug, age 45

21
Bette's Bottomless Handbag

Bette Fullmer was truly a woman to be admired. She had big accomplishments, a huge heart, and a very large purse—which just happened to contain almost every item a person could ever want or need at any given time.

Bette was famous for rummaging through her cavernous handbag to retrieve anything from a measuring spoon to a thimble, a cough drop to a zipper-lock bag, a safety pin to a pocket dictionary. But one of Bette's most surprising handbag contents miraculously appeared after a strenuous hike many years ago, which I share in her daughter's own words:

"We were all setting out to climb Angel's Landing in Zion National Park as a family. Bette took off with her purse.

"I said, 'Mom! Lose the purse.'

"She just laughed and kept walking.

"'Mom,' I continued. 'The purse!'

"At the switchbacks, about fifteen of us sat down, exhausted and parched. Then, out of the great 'black hole' that was Bette's purse, came fifteen diet sodas—all cold and wrapped in tin foil!"

That was the Bette we all knew and loved.

Bette recently passed from this world to the next. Her only daughter, Judi, shared the following sweet tribute at Bette's remarkable funeral:

Mom,

Your gentle guidance has immeasurably influenced all that I have done, all that I do, and all that I will ever do.

Your sweet, sassy spirit is indelibly imprinted on all that I have been, all that I am, and all that I will ever be.

Thus, you are a part of all that I accomplish and all that I become.

And so it is that when I help my neighbor, your helping hand is there also.

When I ease the pain of a friend, she owes a debt to you.

When I show a child a better way, you are the teacher once removed.

Because everything I do reflects the values learned from you.

Any wrong that I right, any heart I may brighten, any gift that I share or burden I may lighten is, in its own small way, a tribute to you, Mom.

Because you gave me life, and, more importantly, lessons in how to live, you are the wellspring from which flows all the good I may achieve in my time here on earth.

For all that you are—and all that I am—thank you.

Thank you for my life.

As you can clearly see, in addition to possessing a bottomless handbag, Bette Fullmer also possessed the limitless love of her loyal daughter. And that's just the sort of blessing this woman lived for . . . and which every mother longs to receive.

The Offering

Example

One that serves as a pattern to be imitated; a model of behavior.

Work hard.

Play hard.

"I really love my mom for leaving a light on for me at night. Even though I'm in college now and I'm gone a lot, that one small thing reminds me that she still cares about me."

David, age 21

22
Hunting for Courage

We have each clung to little fears, and Grace's daughter was no exception. During her entire sixth-grade year, this girl had voiced worry about entering junior high school. "What if my friends all find new friends? What if I can't keep up with my homework for seven different classes? What if I get lost in that big building and never find my way out!" she would ramble on as she walked alongside her mother while shopping for new school clothes.

As August came, it was only natural that Grace's daughter was increasingly more nervous about entering a new phase of her young life. And understandably, she needed to voice her concerns. But Grace began to wonder what she could do as a mother to ease her daughter's troubled heart.

Then the answer hit her . . .

Grace began planning and gathering, plotting and preparing for the pre-junior high mother's mite her daughter would never forget. She visited the school, made an appointment with her daughter's future guidance counselor, and gained permission from the principal to place scavenger hunt clues all around the temporarily empty junior high halls. Then she excitedly went home to get her anxious daughter.

Grace told her tense tween a little white fib, saying she had to attend a quick PTA meeting at the school, but wanted her to come along. Even though this uneasy girl strongly resisted, Grace managed to get her out of the house, into the car, and over to the school. And then that clever mother excused herself for the "PTA meeting" (wink) while her daughter waited uncomfortably in the hallway.

As this girl sat facing a brick wall in her new school, she couldn't help but notice an envelope taped to the center of the wall in front of her with her name typed on the front.

Curiously, she walked toward the envelope, opened it, and carefully read the printed clue inside:

> *Turn to your left*
> *Take twelve large steps*
> *See the note on the door*
> *You'll like what's in store . . .*

With each fun, fresh clue, Grace's daughter found herself at her assigned locker, at the school gym, at the lunchroom, and so on. And since she was alone, she could take her time exploring this unfamiliar school at her own pace. The final clue landed this ever-more-confident girl at her guidance counselor's office where she was greeted with open arms for a one-on-one chat, complete with chocolate-covered caramels and a personalized school calendar.

What might have taken many months to accomplish was realized in a matter of mere minutes with this wise mother's ingenuity and the help of a supportive school staff. And while it did take some planning and effort on this clever mother's part to create an innovative *game* to help calm her daughter's fears, Grace's willingness ultimately paid off in spades!

The Offering

Goodwill

An act or attitude of kindness or benevolence; cheerful acquiescence or willingness.

Model healthy living.

Greet your children with
a cheerful voice.

"My mom did the best she could,
and in my book, that makes her the best."

Rob, age 55

23
Churning Ice Cream

In the small town where I was born, going to the store for things such as milk, veggies, or eggs just wasn't done very often. If you ran out of milk, you simply sent a child over to Morris Ogden's barn to get a fresh gallon from one of his cows. If you needed some beans for dinner, you simply gave your son a bowl and asked him to go out and pick some from the garden, or you sent your daughter down to the cellar for a home-canned bottle. Eggs were easy. You just walked out to the chicken coop and checked the straw nests until you found all of the eggs hiding there. If you ever ran out, your next-door neighbor usually had a few to spare.

But one of my best-loved memories of home-produced food in that quiet little town was making ice cream in our large wooden freezer. With cream from the Ogdens' cows, and fresh strawberries or peaches from our yard, we could whip out some pretty scrumptious desserts in our barrel-shaped churn.

After my mom had packed the crushed ice and salt around the edges of the shiny, clean cylinder containing all of the rich ingredients, my brother and I would each take turns rotating the large metal handle. To be perfectly honest, my mother did most of the work, but we all felt a huge sense of ownership when the finished product was ready to eat.

I'll never forget the first time I noticed that the ice cream purchased from the grocery store didn't quite compare to the awe-inspiring scrumptiousness of our family's homemade brand. Ours was definitely ice cream worth craving. Although the store-bought varieties were generally passable, I quickly realized there was nothing quite like the process of putting that creamy deliciousness together as a family. Churning ice cream at home just made every bite taste a whole lot better.

The Offering

Self-Sufficiency

A modest but adequate scale of living; competency.

OLD-FASHIONED ICE CREAM
(makes 4 quarts)

4 cups sugar

Juice from 4 large lemons

2 quarts plus 2 cups milk, divided

2 cups heavy whipping cream

2 cups crushed fruit, if desired (fresh peaches or strawberries work great)

1. In a large saucepan, melt sugar in 2 cups milk.
2. Add juice from lemons, heavy cream, and rest of milk.
3. Blend in crushed fruit.
4. Freeze in an ice cream freezer following manufacturer's directions.

Hot Fudge Sauce
(yields 2 pints)

½ cup butter

1 (12-ounce) bag semisweet chocolate chips

½ cup light corn syrup

1⅓ cups sugar

Pinch of salt

1⅓ cups evaporated milk

1. Melt butter on low, low heat. Add chocolate chips, continue to melt, stirring constantly. Add corn syrup, sugar, and salt and stir. Add evaporated milk and stir.
2. Turn up heat a bit to medium so mixture will boil softly. Stir constantly. When mixture is gently bubbling, turn back to low heat so mixture will continue to boil gently. Stir with a spatula—constantly turning over. Stir for approximately 6–8 minutes.
3. You can add peanut butter, mint flavor, etc., after sauce has cooked.

Make homemade ice cream together.

Write love notes to your children.

"My mom liked to fold the laundry at the kitchen table
because it was in a central spot in our home.
We had some of our very best talks
around those piles of clothes."

Trish, aged to perfection

24
Jessica's Garden

Jessica was in her early teens when she showed an unusual interest in gardening. She often visited Temple Square in Salt Lake City, where she loved to sit and plan her own future garden, eager for the day when her dreams could become reality. This young woman's astute mother recognized Jessica's budding interest, and out of love for this girl, she chose a four-by-fifteen-foot patch of ground in the backyard that she dedicated just to her.

Throughout high school, while other girls were shopping for the latest fashions, Jessica and her mother were shopping for the perfect peonies. And from her grandmother and others she loved, Jessica gathered plant clippings from which she developed "starts"—each one blossoming with both meaning and beauty in her own private space. That once-barren plot of ground soon became a patchwork of rich textures and colors. It was a living laboratory for growth, industry, and the personal development of a girl who deeply revered the earth. Jessica's garden steadily grew to be a sanctuary of peace and solace for this ambitious, introspective young woman.

Today, growing beautiful things has become more than just a hobby for Jessica.

Her love for gardening has grown into a way of life. With a four-year university degree in ornamental horticulture, Jessica now owns and operates a thriving landscaping business. And the garden she once created and cared for as a youth is now like that in *The Secret Garden*.

This secret garden stands as a tribute to a sensitive mother who recognized and acted upon her daughter's aspirations, even when her initial interest was merely a tiny seed. That wise mother's willingness to help Jessica develop the gifts that were uniquely hers is a testament to the powerful, positive result that *taking action* can bring.

The Offering

Taking Action

The state or process of acting or doing; accomplishing something; influencing.

Forgive yourself.

Forget yourself.

"My friends always like coming over to my house—especially when my mom makes snickerdoodles."

Gretta, age 9

25
Scattering Seashells

Adrianne grew up near Sanibel Island, Florida, where sunshine and seashells are as plentiful as warmhearted people. When she decided to marry, her fiancé had already firmly planted his career in the beautifully green, yet often cloudy state of Washington. So that's where they determined to put down their roots.

As this bright young couple grew their family, Adrianne loved taking her small children back to Florida where they could visit with relatives, soak up the sun, and collect the most interesting seashells imaginable. Her children relished finding sand dollars, small pieces of coral, and colorful shells—just as Adrianne had done as a child.

After one particularly warm and glorious trip to Florida, her days in the state of Washington seemed unbearably short on sunshine, and Adrianne became unbearably short on smiles. The dreariness of so many gray clouds day after day made her homesick for the sunny spot she knew and loved so well.

One mostly clear Monday morning, as she sat trying to muster up enough courage to clean her kitchen, she had a brilliant idea! She hurried into her bedroom, took a bulging bag from her dresser, and began excitedly calling the names of her children—who had been watching television all morning.

"Get your swimsuits on, everybody!" she said with a newfound smile. "We're going to the beach today."

"The beach!" they all yelled excitedly.

Buckets and shovels were speedily packed into the family's minivan and off they went on their spontaneous day trip. When they finally arrived at the beach and started to spread out their water gear, Adrianne's children seemed confused. Not only was it much colder than it had been in Florida, but the brownish sand was covered with rocks.

"Mommy, Mommy! Where are the shells?" cried her youngest, scanning the shoreline.

"Not to worry," said her mother calmly, as she continued unpacking the van. Soon the children were laughing and playing. Adrianne quietly retrieved the bag she had brought from home and began walking toward some large

The Offering

Intense and especially ecstatic or exultant happiness.

boulders not far away, clearing a path as she went. After several minutes, she called back to her kids.

"Hey! Come over here, you guys . . . You've gotta see this!"

Between four large rocks, Adrianne had smoothed out the sand and scattered literally scores of beautiful seashells. It looked like a treasure chest just waiting to be plundered! Her children all squealed at the sight. What could have been a depressing day became a day to remember, simply because my friend decided to smooth the path and prepare the way for a little joy.

Bite your tongue.

Swallow your pride.

"My mom served me breakfast in bed on my birthday for eighteen years straight. It was amazing to know someone loved me that much."

Nick, age 20

26
Ladies in Waiting

f the truth were actually told, a typical mother's motto should read:

"I hurry up . . . and then I wait."

It seems we moms are endlessly waiting—in the carpool lane, at the doctor's office, dentist's office, orthodontist's office, and at the school office. We wait at practices, performances, lessons, and activities. And if we were each lucky enough to be compensated for all of the time we spend waiting for our children, we might be in Tuscany right now, enjoying the balmy Italian breeze!

I have always admired those women who come prepared for their inevitable fate with a book, some work, an organizer, or a journal and pen—for these are the women who can rightly view their "waiting servitude" as time well spent.

When I was a teenager, my own watchful mother used to sit and read at the top of the stairs until I came home at night. I have many other friends whose mothers waited up and read . . . waiting, waiting, waiting for their chicks to return to the nest. But whether we mothers choose to read, knit, pray, or meditate—the really important thing is that *we never stop waiting* or caring for the well-being of our children, whether they're babies, or big guys, or both!

Those familiar words that every young mother hears over and over—"Wait up, Mom! Don't leave me"—may sadly fade from our ears as our little ones grow taller, but they are by no means obsolete just because they're now unspoken.

In fact, our presence and patience may never be more needed than when our children have children of their own.

The Offering

Patience

The capacity, habit, or fact of being patient; bearing provocation with calmness.

Notice the clouds.

Play hopscotch.

"If I could tell my mom only one thing
at the end of the day, I would simply say, 'Thank you.'
Because everything I am today . . . I owe to her."

Kelly, age 37

27
Grandma Jo

oAnne was my neighbor. She was older than I, much wiser than I, and she kindly hired my eight-year-old son to gather her mail and watch over her house while she and her husband were away—which was often. And although this highly charitable woman was already a terrific grandmother to her own four grandchildren, she was quickly adopted by my adoring youngsters and rightly named "Grandma Jo."

Now, our self-proclaimed adoption of Grandma Jo didn't come about because my children were lacking attention from their own splendid grandmothers. Quite the opposite. They were, and still are, very blessed to have two wonderful women they fittingly call "Grandma." But JoAnne became like blood because she always treated our family like her own. She simply loved her way into our hearts. Permanently.

It's been almost thirteen years since we moved from Grandma Jo's neighborhood, but—from that time to this—she hasn't forgotten a holiday, a birthday, a graduation, or a lunch date. In fact, her thoughtful and generous offerings are nothing short of inspirational!

We often receive little cards, letters, e-mails, and goodies, since *giving* is her specialty. But perhaps the most memorable gift she has ever given us is a s'more maker. Much like the quesadilla maker from the previous year, this handy kitchen gadget is uniquely sensational! I mean, *who* in this world is lucky enough to have a s'more maker? Well, we are. Thanks to our very hip and charitable Grandma Jo.

And even though genetics have absolutely nothing to do with our close and loving relationship with this thoughtful and considerate giver, Grandma Jo's legacy of love and generosity will forever be part of our family's heritage. S'mores and all . . .

The Offering

Generosity

Giving abundantly; willingness to give; unselfishness; openhandedness.

OVEN S'MORES

graham crackers
chocolate bars
marshmallows

Place graham crackers on a baking sheet. Place one square of chocolate or a few chocolate chips on each cracker. Place a marshmallow on each piece of chocolate. Place in a preheated 350 degree F. oven for 5 minutes, or just long enough to melt the marshmallow and soften the chocolate. Remove from oven and place another graham cracker on top to make a sandwich.

Bon appétit!

Choose happiness.

Be believing.

"I loved it when my mom would bring a fresh red rose to my ballet recitals. She would give it to me with a great big hug, and I felt just like a prima ballerina."

Grace, age 30

28
A Mother's Might

One calm summer morning, Anne-Marie Barton arrived just a bit late to church and quietly slipped onto the bench where her family was already seated. Her teenage daughter, Sophie, tenderly enveloped her mother with a loving embrace. When the meeting was over, Anne-Marie felt touched when a woman seated behind them said she had never seen such love expressed between a mother and a daughter. This thoughtful woman commented that Sophie's ease in caressing her mother was evidence of their tremendous relationship. And the woman was right.

The very next day, on June 28, 2010, this seventeen-year-old girl was suddenly and unexpectedly called home to that God who gave her life. To say Sophie's death was a shock would be a total understatement. It was unspeakable. To her family, to our community, and to everyone who knew Sophie Rose Barton.

But it was true, just the same.

Completely devastated, this grief-stricken mother found it impossible to believe that in her daughter's ultimate time of need, there had been nothing she could do. Although Anne-Marie had *pleaded* and *prayed* for help as her daughter lay dying from a then-undiagnosed heart defect, nothing came in time to save Sophie. This relentless thought kept Anne-Marie, a highly devoted and capable mother, feeling like she had not done enough, that more could have been done, and that she had let her daughter down.

No words could adequately describe the utter loss she felt, nor the piercing pain in her chest. And yet, with four other children, her heartsick husband, work, and real life ahead, Anne-Marie Barton had to lean on the very phrase she had raised her children to believe when they had each faced difficult obstacles. Her well-rehearsed phrase was: "Feel the fear and do it anyway!"[3]

More than a thousand people gathered to honor this extraordinary young woman who personified goodness and whose music touched our souls. And after Sophie's many friends and family members had shared their fondest thoughts and personal experiences, her parents arose and, with unexpected composure, spoke of the *little things* Sophie had said and done that now meant so very much: her willingness to reach out to those in need, her constant smile, loud laughter, and her abundant collection of cute shoes! They spoke of Sunday dinners on the lawn, of watching family movies, and of Sophie's patriarchal blessing. But most importantly, they spoke of her uncommon bond with their close family and her Father in Heaven.

As I passed the countless white ribbons tied around trees and pillars throughout our community in her honor—I thought not only of sweet Sophie Barton, who was now free from the pain and fears of this fleeting earthly existence. I thought about my brave friend, Anne-Marie, who was digging deeply to "do it anyway."

As she tried to get through the final words while speaking at Sophie's funeral, this sorrow-burdened mother promised to "jump on the trampoline and play hot dice" with her children again soon.

And so will I.

Because I was profoundly inspired by her words, I am also *recommitting*. I'm now riding more bikes, taking more hikes, and relishing daily family life as I haven't in years. Sophie's passing has reaffirmed to me that when all is said and done, it will be those small, simple moments we will each remember . . .

. . . and cherish the most.

The Offering

Renewed Hope

A desire that is newly cherished with anticipation; an expectation grounded in confidence.

Live in the moment.

Make today count.

" . . . but she of her want did cast in all that she had, even all her living."

Mark 12:44

Conclusion: Giving Our All

hat does it mean to give our all? Does it mean we must give until we're totally empty, completely spent, and all used up?

It's no secret that we mothers have a demanding, often exhausting 24/7 job. And for many women, "The joys of motherhood are never fully experienced until the children are all in bed."[4] So, if we want to be completely honest with one another, weighing our own efforts against those of a poor widow who was willing to offer up the very last cent she had might naturally make us feel overwhelmed and intimidated, not inspired!

But we can each find renewed hope, strength, and joy as we *recommit* to giving our all, which is merely our best, as mothers, grandmothers, and leaders, to this incredible rising generation.

We can each defend ourselves against that all-too-familiar feeling that we're not doing enough, that we're not measuring up, and that in "losing ourselves" we are essentially losing our very selves. And we can each take comfort in the fact that by simply trying to give, little by little, we will succeed in making a positive difference—even if we often fall short of our lofty goals.

No mother gives her all—all of the time. It's simply not in any way possible. But like the widow of old, if we merely give what we have—humble though it may be—we will find great peace in feeling we have offered well.

Jeffrey R. Holland reassuringly confirmed, "If you try your best to be the best parent you can be, you will have done all that a human being can do and all that God expects you to do."[5] And in trying to be the very best parents we can be, let us pause often to celebrate and savor our small successes, to delight in the little things we do well, and to lift other nurturers who walk beside us along this bumpy path of parenting.

Why do our smallest efforts matter?

Because even our poorest, most pathetic little offerings can have a profoundly powerful effect upon the lives of those we love! All those teensey, measly, minuscule mother's mites we find ourselves wondering about really do make a positive difference.

Even if our children seldom . . .

if ever . . .

let us know.

Notes

1. This quote is attributed to Maya Angelou in Bob Kelly's *Worth Repeating: More Than 5,000 Classic and Contemporary Quotes* (Grand Rapids, Mich.: Kregel Publications, 2003), 263.
2. http://www.stardate.org/nightsky/meteors/. Accessed on November 12, 2010.
3. Registered trademark of Susan Jeffers, PhD, who wrote *Feel the Fear and Do It Anyway* (New York: Fawcett Books, 1987).
4. Author unknown. Found at http://www.lovethepoem.com/motherpoems/70.htm. Accessed November 12, 2010.
5. Jeffrey R. Holland, "Because She Is a Mother," *Ensign*, May 1997, 129.

The "offerings" definitions are compilations and adaptations from various sources. Many are from www.merriam-webster.com.

Illustration Credits

Believe

UPLIFT

GIVE

OFFER

Love

Affirm

Encourage

Elevate

Inspire

Validate

Share

Believe

UPLIFT

GIVE

OFFER

Love

Affirm

Encourage

Elevate

Inspire

Validate

Share